AMERICAN HOLIDAYS AND CELEBRATIONS

BLACK HISTORY MONTH

Sierra Wilson

LIGHTBOX
openlightbox.com

LIGHTBOX

Go to **www.openlightbox.com** and enter this book's unique code.

ACCESS CODE

LBXF8845

Lightbox is an all-inclusive digital solution for the teaching and learning of curriculum topics in an original, groundbreaking way. Lightbox is based on National Curriculum Standards.

LIGHTBOX SUPPLEMENTARY RESOURCES

SHARE
Share titles within your Learning Management System (LMS) or Library Circulation System

CURRICULUM
Find national and state curriculum correlations

CITATION
Create bibliographical references following APA, CMOS, and MLA styles

STANDARD FEATURES OF LIGHTBOX

AUDIO High-quality narration using text-to-speech system

ACTIVITIES Printable PDFs that can be emailed and graded

SLIDESHOWS Pictorial overviews of key concepts

VIDEOS Embedded high-definition video clips

WEBLINKS Curated links to external, child-safe resources

TRANSPARENCIES Step-by-step layering of maps, diagrams, charts, and timelines

INTERACTIVE MAPS Interactive maps and aerial satellite imagery

QUIZZES Ten multiple-choice questions that are automatically graded and emailed for teacher assessment

KEY WORDS Matching key concepts to their definitions

This title is part of our Lightbox digital subscription

Lightbox Grades 3–5 Subscription
ISBN 978-1-5105-5424-5

Access hundreds of Lightbox titles with our digital subscription. Sign up for a **FREE** subscription trial at **www.openlightbox.com/trial**

The digital components of this book are guaranteed to stay active for at least five years from the date of publication.

AMERICAN HOLIDAYS AND CELEBRATIONS

BLACK HISTORY MONTH

CONTENTS

slavery interrupted

Mufaro's Beautiful Daughters

What Is Black History Month?

Black History Month is a **heritage** month in the United States. The month of February is set apart as a time to study and reflect on Black history and the contributions of Black Americans. Before the creation of Black History Month, Black history was not widely studied in the United States. Over the past hundred years and more, the study and appreciation of Black history has grown. Black History Month is now a vibrant celebration throughout the country.

During Black History Month, a variety of events are held to showcase the achievements of Black Americans. Museums put together special exhibits devoted to Black history. Arts groups stage music and dance performances centered around Black culture. Parades and festivals are held across the country to celebrate.

Every year, the White House holds a reception in honor of Black History Month. Black leaders and community members are among those who attend.

Black History Month Origins

Black History Month began as the dream of an African American historian named Carter G. Woodson. Woodson's goal was to encourage the study of Black history. To do this, he founded an organization and **journal** focused on Black history. In February 1926, his organization held the first official Black History Week, then called Negro History Week.

Across the United States, schools and other groups studied Black history and organized Black history clubs. Soon, the enthusiasm for Black history grew, and celebrations began lasting the entire month of February. Many schools began teaching aspects of Black history all year, even though some faced opposition.

Timeline

Summer 1915

Carter G. Woodson takes part in a national celebration marking the 50th anniversary of **emancipation** in the United States. Thousands of people come to Chicago from across the country to see exhibits about the progress Black Americans have made since gaining their freedom.

September 9, 1915

Woodson helps found the Association for the Study of Negro Life and History, now known as the Association for the Study of African American Life and History, to promote the study of Black history.

1924

Woodson encourages his friends and colleagues to help spread the word about Black American achievements. They create Negro History and Literature Week, which is later renamed Negro Achievement Week.

Finally, in 1976, Black History Month was officially recognized by President Gerald Ford. Ten years later, **Congress** passed a law designating February as Black History Month. The president at the time, Ronald Reagan, gave a speech to commemorate the event. He noted that Black History Month was a time to recognize Black Americans' struggle for freedom as well as their many achievements and contributions. Today, Black History Month is also celebrated in Canada, Germany, the United Kingdom, and several other countries.

As part of 1984's Black History Month, President Reagan unveiled a stamp honoring Carter G. Woodson and his efforts to promote the study of Black history.

February 1926

The first Negro History Week is announced. It is organized by Woodson's association and held during the second week of February, to coincide with the birthdays of Abraham Lincoln and Frederick Douglass.

February 1976

President Gerald Ford officially recognizes February as Black History Month. All Americans are encouraged to learn about the impact and achievements of Black Americans.

2023

Black History Month's theme is "Black Resistance." It focuses on those who have fought to end Black **oppression**.

Important People

Carter G. Woodson is known as the "father of Black history." He was born in 1875 to parents who had been slaves. Raised in poverty, he did not have the chance to attend high school until he was 20 years old. After finishing his schooling in just two years, Woodson went on to earn several college degrees. He was the second Black American to graduate with a PhD from Harvard University. Woodson spent his life working to study, honor, and share the importance of Black history and culture with others.

When Woodson decided to create the first Negro History Week, he chose a week in February as the time to hold it. This week included the birthdays of two men who were prominent in the fight for African American rights. Frederick Douglass had long campaigned against slavery. Abraham Lincoln, the country's 16th president, was responsible for the **Emancipation Proclamation**. Black Americans had been honoring these two birthdays since the 19th century.

CHAMPIONS OF FREEDOM

Frederick Douglass

Born February 1818
Birthplace Talbot County, Maryland
Education Self-taught
Died February 20, 1895

Abraham Lincoln

Born February 12, 1809
Birthplace Hodgenville, Kentucky
Education Self-taught
Died April 15, 1865

Carter G. Woodson Memorial Park opened in 2015, not far from Woodson's home in Washington, DC. The park features a bronze statue of Woodson seated on a stone memorial.

Black History Month Celebrations

Woodson's week of celebration was an immediate success. Schools were eager to get involved. Students recited speeches, participated in essay contests, and staged plays and **pageants** about aspects of Black history. Communities also participated by holding a variety of cultural events. Over time, the week-long celebration was extended to a full month.

Today, people continue to participate in these types of activities each Black History Month. They also work to find new ways to commemorate the occasion. Since 1928, the Association for the Study of African American Life and History has announced an annual theme for each. This has brought attention to specific issues that Black Americans have faced in the past and continue to face today. Recent themes have included African Americans and the Vote and African Americans in Times of War. Black History Month encourages people to honor the past while looking for ways to improve the future.

Parades are a popular way to celebrate Black History Month. They take place in communities across the nation.

Celebrations Around the World

Canada

In June, Canadians celebrate National Indigenous History Month to learn about, recognize, and celebrate the culture and history of the country's Indigenous Peoples.

South Africa

In April, South Africans celebrate Freedom Month. This is a time to remember the inequality and racism of South Africa's past. It is also a time to celebrate progress and to honor the sacrifices made to achieve freedom and **democracy**.

Australia

At the end of May, Australia holds its National **Reconciliation** Week. This week is meant to show respect for the relationships the country has with its Indigenous Peoples and to encourage people to take their own steps toward reconciliation.

Celebrating Today

People celebrate Black History Month in many ways. Some visit museums and historic sites focused on Black history. Locations such as the National **Civil Rights** Museum, in Memphis, Tennessee, and the Martin Luther King, Jr. National Historical Park, in Atlanta, Georgia, typically hold special events and exhibits during this month.

Martin Luther King, Jr. was a key member of the civil rights movement, a campaign focused on ending unfair laws and practices against Black Americans. One of his best-known contributions to the movement, and the history of the United States, occurred at the March on Washington on August 28, 1963. In his "I Have a Dream" speech, King called for a future where people of all races live in harmony.

People also take the time to read books and watch films about the Black American experience. Music is often a big part of Black History Month, with people enjoying jazz, blues, and hip-hop performances. Some see Black History Month as a time to show their support for local businesses. They may eat at a restaurant or shop in a store owned by Black Americans.

Bookstores often hold special events during Black History Month, inviting Black writers to read excerpts from their books and sign copies for interested book lovers.

BLACK AMERICANS IN BUSINESS

141,000
Black-owned businesses in the United States

3%
of all U.S. businesses

$141 billion
in sales per year

Black History Month in the United States

Black History Month is celebrated across the United States in cities and towns of all sizes. This map shows a few of the events that take place in different parts of the country during Black History Month.

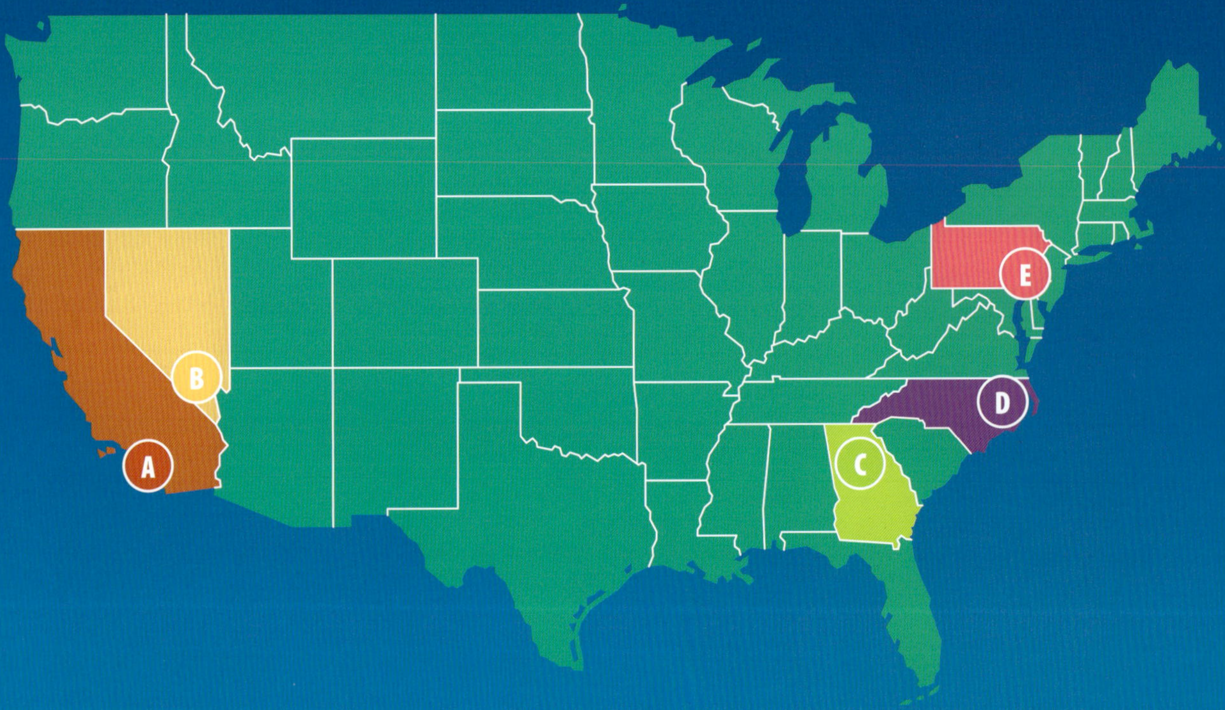

A California Los Angeles

B Nevada Las Vegas

C Georgia Atlanta

D North Carolina Raleigh

E Pennsylvania Philadelphia

A Los Angeles

Los Angeles hosts the Pan African Film and Arts Festival during Black History Month. One of the country's largest Black film festivals, it screens more than 200 films by or about Black people from around the world each year.

B Las Vegas

Every February, Springs Preserve holds its Black History Month Festival. This family-friendly event features cultural dancing, music, and food, as well as arts and crafts, photo exhibits, and educational presentations.

C Atlanta

One of the largest Black History Month celebrations in the Southeast is Atlanta's Black History Month Parade. The parade includes marching bands, dancers, floats, and more, with a focus on celebrating Black culture.

D Raleigh

For more than 20 years, the North Carolina Museum of History has kicked off Black History Month with its African American Cultural Celebration. The event hosts performances, talks, and films from prominent members of the Black community.

E Philadelphia

Philadelphia has been holding its African American Children's Book Fair during Black History Month for more than 30 years. Considered one of the oldest and largest African American book fairs, it features authors and illustrators from across the country.

Black History Month Symbols

Black History Month is a time to celebrate the achievements of Black Americans. It is also a time to reflect on the struggles and challenges Black Americans have faced and continue to face today. Special colors and symbols play a part in both celebrating and remembering during Black History Month.

Black History Colors

The official colors for Black History Month are black, red, green, and yellow. These colors come from the Pan-African flag and the Ethiopian flag. Black symbolizes the Black race. Red symbolizes the bloodshed of lost Black lives. Green symbolizes the lush vegetation of Africa. Yellow symbolizes justice, hope, and equality.

The Pan-African flag is a common sight at marches and parades that promote Black culture and causes.

Raised Fist

A raised fist is a symbol of Black pride, unity, and commitment to fighting injustice. A raised fist was used as a symbol during the civil rights movement. It continues to be used today by movements such as **Black Lives Matter**. Throughout history, a raised fist has meant strength, solidarity, and perseverance.

Sankofa Bird

The Sankofa bird symbol originated in West Africa. A bird is shown facing forward but looking backward to take an egg from its back. This image is said to portray the goal of Black History Month, which is to reflect on the past while moving toward the future.

Each part of the Sankofa bird has a special meaning. The body represents the past, while the head stands for the present. The egg is the future.

A Poem to Remember

Throughout American history, Black Americans have created powerful songs and poems that have impacted thought and culture. Amanda Gorman, a young African American poet and the first National Youth Poet Laureate, read her poem about Black history and American history, "The Hill We Climb," at President Joseph Biden's **inauguration**. Below is a section from that poem.

"...And so we lift our gaze, not to what stands between us
but what stands before us.
We close the divide because we know, to put our future first,
we must first put our differences aside.
We lay down our arms
so we can reach out our arms
to one another.
We seek harm to none and harmony for all.
Let the globe, if nothing else, say this is true:
That even as we grieved, we grew;
that even as we hurt, we hoped;
that even as we tired, we tried;
that we'll forever be tied together, victorious..."

Write Your Own Poem

Poetry is a wonderful way to express thoughts and feelings. There are different ways to write a poem. Some poems have a specific structure. Many poems rhyme, while others sound like natural speech. One fun and simple type of poem is called an acrostic.

1

Choose a word to focus on. The word could be a name, place, or important idea.

2

Start your poem by writing one letter from the word on each line of a page, moving down vertically.

3

Next, write a word or phrase that starts with the letter on each line. For example, if you chose the word "winter," your first word or phrase would start with "w."

4

When you have written words or phrases for each line, practice reading your new poem aloud to yourself. If you want to, you can change some of the words or phrases.

5

Read your poem aloud to someone else. Poetry is meant to be shared and enjoyed.

TIP

When creating your poem, choose your words thoughtfully. Poems often use sensory language that brings to mind sights, scents, sounds, tastes, and feelings. Poems also use active, specific verbs such as "crackle," "whisper," or "tiptoe."

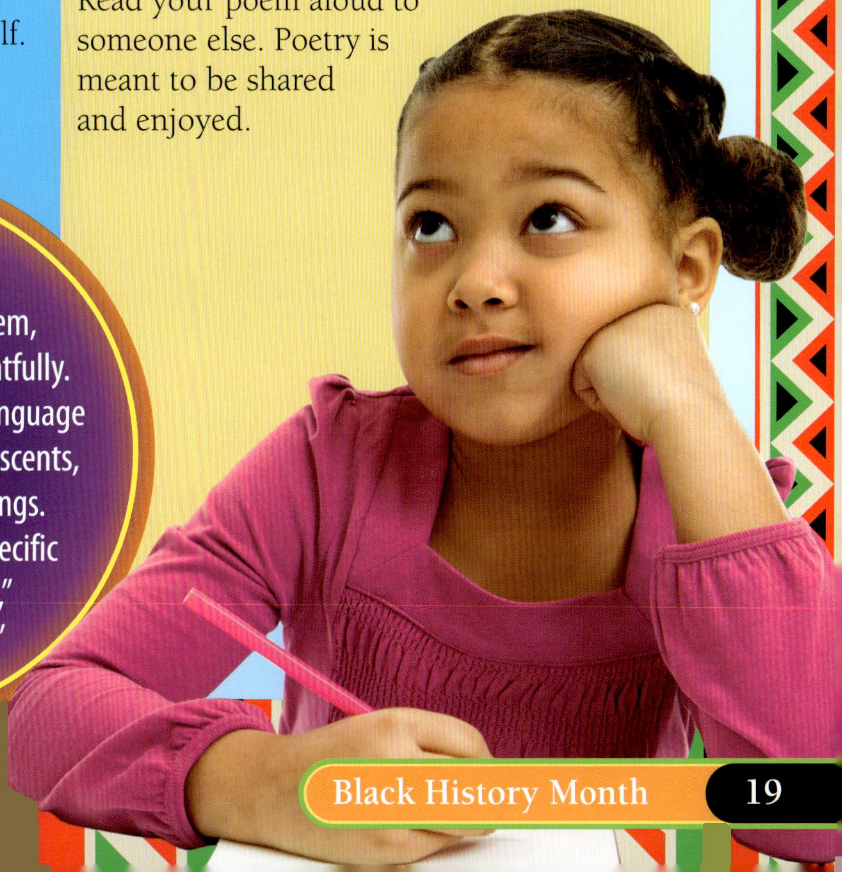

Making a Traffic Light

Part of Black History Month is celebrating the accomplishments and inventions of Black Americans. A Black American inventor named Garrett Morgan invented the three-position traffic light. This traffic light craft uses the four colors of Black History Month.

Materials Needed

4 sheets of construction paper (black, red, yellow, and green)

A pencil

A cup

Scissors

Glue

Directions

1. Use the cup to trace three circles in a row on the black paper.
2. Cut or tear small pieces of the red, yellow, and green papers.
3. Glue the paper pieces onto the circles to fill them in. Make sure to arrange the colors in order. The red circle is at the top. The yellow circle is in the middle. The green circle is at the bottom.
4. Hang up your traffic light as a Black History Month decoration!

Making Red Beans and Rice

Red beans and rice is a popular dish to make during Black History Month. Originating in the state of Louisiana, it is considered soul food. This is food that is traditionally prepared and eaten by African Americans in the southern United States.

Ingredients Needed

- 1 tablespoon (15 milliliters) olive oil
- 1 cup (237 mL) diced onion
- 1 cup (237 mL) diced green bell pepper
- 1 tablespoon (15 mL) minced garlic
- 1 ½ teaspoons (7.5 mL) ground cumin
- 1 ½ teaspoons (7.5 mL) dried oregano
- 1 14.5-ounce can (430 mL) chicken broth
- ½ cup (120 mL) instant brown rice, uncooked
- 2 15-ounce cans (450 mL) red kidney beans, drained and rinsed

Materials Needed

Stovetop

Wooden spoon

Small pot

Directions

1. With an adult's help, heat the olive oil in a small pot on medium heat. Cook and stir the onion in the pot for 5 minutes.
2. Add the green peppers. Cook and stir for 5 more minutes.
3. Add the garlic, cumin, and oregano. Cook and stir for 1 minute.
4. Mix in the rice and broth. Stir well. Then, cover the pan and let it simmer for 10 minutes.
5. Stir in the beans. Cover and simmer for 5 more minutes.
6. Enjoy!

Black History Month Quiz

1 When was Black History Month officially recognized?

2 Which historian had the idea to celebrate Black history in February?

3 Whose birthdays were contained within Negro History Week?

4 Who was the first National Youth Poet Laureate?

5 Who invented the three-color traffic light?

6 What are the four colors of Black History Month?

7 Which country celebrates National Indigenous History Month each June?

8 When did Black History Month start having themes?

9 Where did red beans and rice originate?

10 Which city hosts the Pan African Film and Arts Festival?

ANSWERS: 1. 1976 2. Carter G. Woodson 3. Frederick Douglass and Abraham Lincoln 4. Amanda Gorman 5. Garrett Morgan 6. Black, red, green, and yellow 7. Canada 8. 1928 9. Louisiana 10. Los Angeles

Key Words

Black Lives Matter: a movement dedicated to fighting racism and anti-Black violence

civil rights: guarantees of equal social opportunities and equal protection under the law, regardless of race, religion, or other personal traits

Congress: the branch of the U.S. government that makes laws

democracy: a form of government in which the people hold the power, either directly or through elected representatives

emancipation: the process of being set free from slavery

Emancipation Proclamation: an 1863 document that declared all slaves in the American South to be free

heritage: a cultural aspect that has been passed down through generations

inauguration: a ceremony to start the term of a new president

journal: a magazine that deals with a particular subject

oppression: the exercise of authority in a cruel or unjust manner

pageants: public performances in which actors often wear costumes

reconciliation: an ongoing process of establishing and maintaining respectful relationships with Indigenous Peoples

Index

LIGHTBOX

SUPPLEMENTARY RESOURCES

Click on the plus icon found in the bottom left corner of each spread to open additional teacher resources.

- Download and print the book's quizzes and activities
- Access curriculum correlations
- Explore additional web applications that enhance the Lightbox experience

LIGHTBOX DIGITAL TITLES
Packed full of integrated media

VIDEOS

INTERACTIVE MAPS

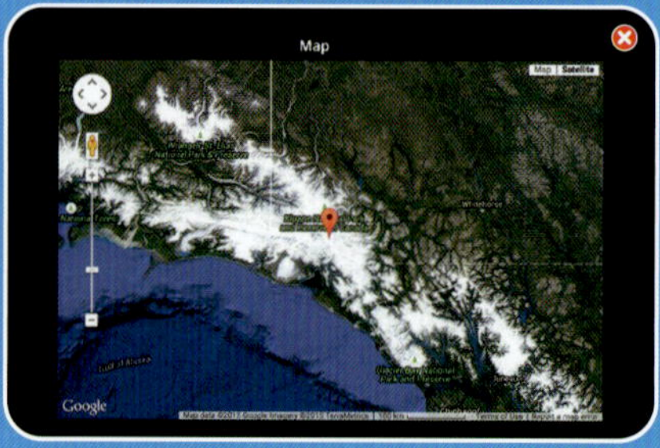

WEBLINKS

SLIDESHOWS

QUIZZES

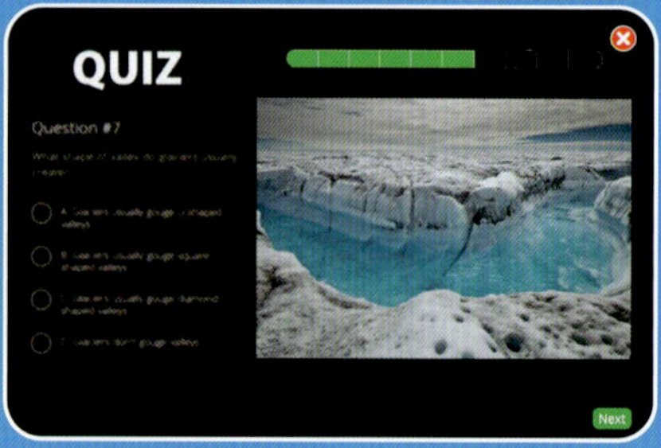

OPTIMIZED FOR

- ✔ TABLETS
- ✔ SMART BOARDS
- ✔ COMPUTERS
- ✔ AND MUCH MORE!

Published by Lightbox Learning Inc.
276 5th Avenue, Suite 704 #917
New York, NY 10001
Website: www.openlightbox.com

Project Coordinator Heather Kissock
Designer Terry Paulhus

Library of Congress Control Number: 2023939837

ISBN 978-1-5105-6690-3 (hardcover)
ISBN 978-1-5105-6691-0 (multi-user eBook)

Printed in Guangzhou, China
1 2 3 4 5 6 7 8 9 0 27 26 25 24 23

062023
111022

Photo Credits
Every reasonable effort has been made to trace ownership and to obtain permission to reprint copyright material. The publisher would be pleased to have any errors or omissions brought to its attention so that they may be corrected in subsequent printings. The publisher acknowledges Getty Images, Alamy, Dreamstime, Shutterstock, and Wikimedia as its primary image suppliers for this title.